Use at least 11 of your spelling words in a short c
all spelling words used in the story.

Spelling Test

Your Answers	Correct Spelling If Incorrect
1	1
2	2
3	3
4	4
5	5
6	6
7	7
8	8
9	9
10	10
11	11
12	12
13	13
14	14
15	15
16	16
17	17
18	18
19	19
20	20

Extra Credit Spelling Words
Scramble

Name: _____

Date: _____

Let's put your puzzle solving skills to the test. Try unscrambling the words using the words in the box.

advisory	abandon	appreciate	amiable	academy	arraignment
avocado	advice	Binoculars	aircraft	argued	arthritis
accident					

1. naoabdn   _ b _ n _ _ _

2. mcaadey   _ _ _ d _ _ y

3. aectcidn   _ _ _ _ d e _ _

4. decvai   a _ _ _ _ e

5. drayvios   a _ _ i _ _ _ _

6. rarcafit   _ _ r _ r _ _ _

7. bmailae   a _ _ _ b _ _

8. icertpapea   _ _ _ _ e _ _ _ t e

9. adregu   _ _ g _ e _

10. rnaengaimrt   _ _ _ _ i _ _ m _ _ t

11. irhistatr   _ _ _ _ r _ _ i _

12. odcavao   _ v _ _ a _ _

13. anubiloscr   _ _ n _ _ u _ _ _ s

Write sentences using words from above:

1. ....

2. ....

3. ....

Use at least 9 of your spelling words in a short creative story. Underline all spelling words used in the story.

Spelling Test

Your Answers	Correct Spelling If Incorrect
1	1
2	2
3	3
4	4
5	5
6	6
7	7
8	8
9	9
10	10
11	11
12	12
13	13
14	14
15	15
16	16
17	17
18	18
19	19
20	20

Extra Credit Spelling Words
Scramble

Name: _____

Date: _____

Let's put your puzzle solving skills to the test. Try unscrambling the words using the words in the box.

bookshelves	cardigan	candidate	category	clearly	collision
broccoli	chameleon	Cologne	civilized	cinnamon	chauffeur
catastrophe	coffee				

1. ebvlosehsko   b _ o _ _ h _ _ _ _ _

2. bcclioor   b r _ _ _ _ _ _

3. andtedica   c _ _ _ _ _ a _ _

4. raagcnid   _ _ _ _ _ _ a n

5. athetcasrpo   _ _ t _ s t _ _ _ _ _

6. garctyoe   _ _ _ _ g _ r _

7. ehoelanmc   _ h _ m _ _ _ _ _

8. urcefhfau   c h _ _ _ _ _ _ _

9. macninon   _ i _ n _ _ _ _

10. vdeiziicl   c _ _ _ _ _ z _ _

11. yllaecr   _ _ _ _ r l _

12. efcofe   c _ f _ _ _

13. nsocliilo   _ _ l _ _ _ _ _ n

14. lcoegno   _ _ _ _ g n _

Write sentences using words from above:

. ...

. ...

. ...

Use at least 14 of your spelling words in a short creative story. Underline all spelling words used in the story.

Spelling Test

Your Answers	Correct Spelling If Incorrect
1	1
2	2
3	3
4	4
5	5
6	6
7	7
8	8
9	9
10	10
11	11
12	12
13	13
14	14
15	15
16	16
17	17
18	18
19	19
20	20

Extra Credit Spelling Words
Scramble

Name: _____

Date: _____

Let's put your puzzle solving skills to the test. Try unscrambling the words using the words in the box.

companion	committing	competitive	curriculum	contaminate	counterfeit
colonel	controlled	combination	competition	completely	Custodian
commitment					

1. oolelnc   c _ _ _ _ _ l

2. botiaincmon   _ _ _ b i _ _ _ _ _ n

3. icmttemmon   _ o m m _ _ _ _ _ _

4. ttmiincmgo   _ _ _ _ _ t t i _ _

5. nioncmapo   _ _ _ _ a _ _ o _

6. ictmotnpoei   c _ _ _ e t _ _ _ _ _

7. ceimteviopt   _ _ _ p _ _ _ t _ v _

8. pyoctmelle   _ _ _ p _ e _ e _ _

9. aecntoatnim   c _ _ t a _ _ _ _ _ _

10. cdllonorte   _ o _ _ _ _ _ _ e d

11. ucrteeftoin   _ o u _ _ _ _ _ _ i _

12. umucrculir   _ _ _ _ i _ u _ u _

13. otduacsin   C _ _ _ _ _ _ a _

Write sentences using words from above:

1. ....

2. ....

3. ....

Use at least 7 of your spelling words in a short creative story. Underline all spelling words used in the story.

_____

_____

_____

_____

_____

_____

_____

_____

_____

_____

_____

_____

_____

_____

_____

_____

_____

_____

_____

_____

Spelling Test

Your Answers	Correct Spelling If Incorrect
1	1
2	2
3	3
4	4
5	5
6	6
7	7
8	8
9	9
10	10
11	11
12	12
13	13
14	14
15	15
16	16
17	17
18	18
19	19
20	20

Extra Credit Spelling Words
Scramble

Name: _____

Date: _____

et's put your puzzle solving skills to the test. Try unscrambling the words using the words in the box.

dictator	Effect	dependent	dictionary	disable	disgusted
discourage	economy	deprive	disruptive	disrespect	disaster
despondent	decrease				

. eadecers   d _ _ _ _ a _ _   8. astdiser   _ _ _ _ s _ e _

. eendetndp   _ e _ _ _ d _ _ _   9. drcieguaos   _ _ _ c o _ r _ _ _

. epeirdv   d e _ _ _ _ _   10. tuisdsegd   _ _ _ g _ _ _ e _

. noenpsddte   _ e _ _ o _ _ e _ _   11. cseterspid   _ _ s _ e _ _ _ c _

. triocatd   _ _ _ _ a _ _ r   12. dvtipieurs   _ _ s _ _ p t _ _ _

. diriyatcno   _ i _ _ _ o _ _ r _   13. oceomyn   e _ _ _ o _ _

. adlsibe   _ _ _ a _ l _   14. feceft   E _ _ _ _ t

Write sentences using words from above:

_____

_____

_____

Use at least 8 of your spelling words in a short creative story. Underline all spelling words used in the story.

_____

_____

_____

_____

_____

_____

_____

_____

_____

_____

_____

_____

_____

_____

_____

_____

_____

_____

_____

_____

Spelling Test

Your Answers		Correct Spelling If Incorrect	
1		1	
2		2	
3		3	
4		4	
5		5	
6		6	
7		7	
8		8	
9		9	
10		10	
11		11	
12		12	
13		13	
14		14	
15		15	
16		16	
17		17	
18		18	
19		19	
20		20	

Extra Credit Spelling Words
Scramble

Name: _____

Date: _____

et's put your puzzle solving skills to the test. Try unscrambling the words using the words in the box.

favorite	elastic	expand	fierce	except	errands
exotic	embarrass	especially	Formally	extinguish	evaluate
explore	examination				

. elsacti   e _ _ _ _ i _

. rsmrsaabe   _ _ b _ _ _ _ s _

. rasdern   _ r _ _ n _ _

. pascilelye   _ s p _ _ _ _ _ _ y

. vaeeatlu   _ _ _ _ u _ _ e

. ietnianoxma   e _ _ _ _ _ a _ _ _ n

. cetxpe   e x _ _ _ _

8. xeotic   _ _ o _ _ c

9. dxpean   _ _ _ a n _

10. rpelxeo   e _ _ _ _ _ e

11. snegiithxu   _ _ t _ n _ _ _ _ h

12. vfeatiro   f _ _ _ _ i _ _

13. eficre   _ i _ _ _ e

14. flymarlo   _ _ _ m _ _ _ y

rite sentences using words from above:

_____

_____

_____

_____

Use at least 12 of your spelling words in a short creative story. Underline all spelling words used in the story.

_____

_____

_____

_____

_____

_____

_____

_____

_____

_____

_____

_____

_____

_____

_____

_____

_____

_____

_____

Spelling Test

Your Answers	Correct Spelling If Incorrect
1	1
2	2
3	3
4	4
5	5
6	6
7	7
8	8
9	9
10	10
11	11
12	12
13	13
14	14
15	15
16	16
17	17
18	18
19	19
20	20

Extra Credit Spelling Words
Scramble

Name: _____

Date: _____

Let's put your puzzle solving skills to the test. Try unscrambling the words using the words in the box.

gruesome	general	homemade	formerly	herd	homage
haggle	headache	Hospitable	gazelle	harass	hilarious
grim	heirloom				

. rloemfry   _ _ r _ _ _ _ y

. gazllee   g _ _ _ _ l _

. rlnegea   _ e _ e _ _ _

. rgim   _ _ _ m

. megseuro   _ r _ _ s _ _ _

. aglhge   _ _ _ _ l e

. haassr   _ a _ _ s _

8. dahaceeh   _ e _ _ a _ _ _

9. iehlmroo   _ _ _ r l _ _ _

10. rhde   h _ _ _

11. siaihorlu   _ _ _ _ _ i _ u _

12. mehago   _ _ m _ _ e

13. heammeod   _ o m _ _ _ _ _

14. apohtibsle _ _ _ _ i _ a b _ _

Write sentences using words from above:

_____

_____

_____

Use at least 10 of your spelling words in a short creative story. Underline all spelling words used in the story.

Spelling Test

Your Answers	Correct Spelling If Incorrect
1	1
2	2
3	3
4	4
5	5
6	6
7	7
8	8
9	9
10	10
11	11
12	12
13	13
14	14
15	15
16	16
17	17
18	18
19	19
20	20

Extra Credit Spelling Words
Scramble

Name: _____

Date: _____

et's put your puzzle solving skills to the test. Try unscrambling the words using the words in the box.

hostel	lagoon	identity	indictment	imitation	hospital
incumbent	inherit	laboratory	Lieutenant	hybrid	introduction
juvenile					

. aphtlsio _ _ s p _ _ _ _

. lothes _ o _ _ _ l

. hbidyr _ y _ _ i _

. iittedny _ d _ _ _ i _ _

. iittoaimn _ _ _ _ _ t _ _ n

. mictnenub i n _ _ _ _ _ _ _

. iitcmdtnen _ _ d _ c _ _ _ n _

. trinieh i _ h _ _ _ _

. itroiudonnct _ _ _ _ o _ u _ t _ _ _

0. leujneiv _ _ _ e n _ _ _

1. aortabroyl _ _ _ _ _ a t o _ _

2. ganool _ _ _ o o _

3. lenaituetn _ i _ _ t _ _ a _ _

Use at least 5 of your spelling words in a short creative story. Underline all spelling words used in the story.

_____

_____

_____

_____

_____

_____

_____

_____

_____

_____

_____

_____

_____

_____

_____

_____

_____

_____

Spelling Test

Your Answers	Correct Spelling If Incorrect
1	1
2	2
3	3
4	4
5	5
6	6
7	7
8	8
9	9
10	10
11	11
12	12
13	13
14	14
15	15
16	16
17	17
18	18
19	19
20	20

Extra Credit Spelling Words
Scramble

Name: _____

Date: _____

et's put your puzzle solving skills to the test. Try unscrambling the words using the words in the box.

machinery	medicine	memorize	meringue	mellow	material
mathematics	Microwave	measles	maintenance	meticulous	meteorology
luxurious	memories				

. ruuiusxol   _ _ _ _ r i _ _ _   8. mwlloe   m _ _ l _ _

. yeaimhcrn   m _ _ _ _ _ _ r _   9. smiermoe   m e _ _ _ _ _ _

. mnnteancaei _ _ i _ _ _ n a _ _ _   10. mmzrieeo   _ _ m _ r _ _ _

. meiaartl   _ _ t e _ _ _ _   11. gimeuner   _ e _ _ _ _ u _

. tiseamtmhac _ _ _ h _ m _ t _ _ _ 12. mrgeolyooet m _ _ _ _ _ r _ l _ _ _

. maelsse   _ e _ s _ _ _   13. cemstluoui _ _ t i _ _ _ _ u _

. miceined   _ e _ i _ _ _ _   14. eorwicvma   _ _ _ _ _ _ a _ e

rite sentences using words from above:

_____

_____

_____

_____

Use at least 16 of your spelling words in a short creative story. Underline all spelling words used in the story.

Spelling Test

Your Answers	Correct Spelling If Incorrect
1	1
2	2
3	3
4	4
5	5
6	6
7	7
8	8
9	9
10	10
11	11
12	12
13	13
14	14
15	15
16	16
17	17
18	18
19	19
20	20

Use at least 14 of your spelling words in a short creative story. Underline all spelling words used in the story.

Extra Credit Spelling Words Scramble

Name: _____

Date: _____

Let's put your puzzle solving skills to the test. Try unscrambling the words using the words in the box.

nonstop	mispronunciation	newsstand	nonessential	Noteworthy	multiple
murky	nonexistent	nimble	mortified	migratory	niece
mosquito	mull				

1. mtyragoir   _ _ g r _ _ _ _ _

2. uosntrioinmpcnai   _ _ _ p _ _ _ _ n _ _ _ t _ _ n

3. irmoitfde   _ _ r _ i _ _ _ _

4. qsutoimo   m _ _ _ _ _ t _

5. lulm   _ _ l _

6. tlpueilm   _ _ _ t _ p _ _

7. urymk   _ u _ _ _

8. ndetansws   _ e _ _ _ _ _ _ d

9. necei   _ i _ _ _

10. eblnmi   _ i _ b _ _

11. nleniaontsse   _ _ n _ _ _ e _ _ _ _ l

12. enntsxoietn   _ _ _ _ _ i s _ _ n _

13. onontsp   _ _ _ _ t o _

14. hetotnyrow   N _ _ _ _ o _ _ h _

Use at least 17 of your spelling words in a short creative story. Underline all spelling words used in the story.

Extra Credit Spelling Words
Scramble

Name: _____

Date: _____

Let's put your puzzle solving skills to the test. Try unscrambling the words using the words in the box.

participate	overwhelming	pending	Perjury	official	penguin
operation	parallel	opinion	orangutan	objective	perceived
pamper	pendulum				

jtboevcei   _ b _ _ _ t _ _ _

fcofliia   _ f _ i _ _ _ _

eiarnpoto   _ p _ _ a _ _ _ _

pnionoi   _ p _ _ _ _ n

orntuaagn   _ _ _ _ g _ _ a _

gheoienmvwlr   _ _ _ _ w _ _ _ m i _ _

preamp   _ a m _ _ _

allrlpae   _ _ _ a _ l _ _

pcratiaepti   _ _ _ t i _ _ p _ _ _

0. npdeing   p e _ _ _ _ _

1. pdueunml   _ e _ d _ _ _ _

2. guienpn   _ _ _ _ u i _

3. edecvprei   _ _ _ c _ _ _ e _

4. yurjepr   _ _ _ j _ _ y

Use at least 5 of your spelling words in a short creative story. Underline all spelling words used in the story.

_____

_____

_____

_____

_____

_____

_____

_____

_____

_____

_____

_____

_____

_____

_____

_____

_____

_____

_____

Spelling Test

Your Answers		**Correct Spelling If Incorrect**
1		1
2		2
3		3
4		4
5		5
6		6
7		7
8		8
9		9
10		10
11		11
12		12
13		13
14		14
15		15
16		16
17		17
18		18
19		19
20		20

Use at least 7 of your spelling words in a short creative story. Underline all spelling words used in the story.

Spelling Test

Your Answers	Correct Spelling If Incorrect
1	1
2	2
3	3
4	4
5	5
6	6
7	7
8	8
9	9
10	10
11	11
12	12
13	13
14	14
15	15
16	16
17	17
18	18
19	19
20	20

Use at least 12 of your spelling words in a short creative story. Underline all spelling words used in the story.

Extra Credit Spelling Words
Scramble

Name: _____

Date: _____

Let's put your puzzle solving skills to the test. Try unscrambling the words using the words in the box.

persistent	pneumonia	pleasant	poised	Proceed	preservation
pigeon	probably	perturbing	ponder	pique	principal
precious					

esnripsett   _ _ _ _ _ s t _ _ t

etrurpgnib   p _ _ _ u _ _ _ n _

negoip   _ _ g e _ _

pquei   _ i _ _ _

telaspan   _ _ _ _ _ a n _

eomauinpn   p _ _ u _ _ _ _ _

seoidp   _ _ i _ e _

ronepd   _ o _ d _ _

eosrpicu   p _ _ _ _ o _ _

). naorrtiespev   _ _ _ s e _ _ _ _ i _ _

. ncplipari   _ _ _ n _ i _ _ _

. bpolabry   _ _ o _ _ b _ _

. eecdrop   _ _ _ _ e e _

Use at least 10 of your spelling words in a short creative story. Underline
all spelling words used in the story.

Spelling Test

Your Answers		Correct Spelling If Incorrect	
1		1	
2		2	
3		3	
4		4	
5		5	
6		6	
7		7	
8		8	
9		9	
10		10	
11		11	
12		12	
13		13	
14		14	
15		15	
16		16	
17		17	
18		18	
19		19	
20		20	

Use at least 8 of your spelling words in a short creative story. Underline all spelling words used in the story.

_____

_____

_____

_____

_____

_____

_____

_____

_____

_____

_____

_____

_____

_____

_____

_____

_____

_____

_____

_____

Extra Credit Spelling Words
Scramble

Name: _____

Date: _____

It's put your puzzle solving skills to the test. Try unscrambling the words using the words in the box.

publicity	prosecuted	provisions	recommend	Recruit	projector
received	productivity	recognition	reality	recede	prophecy
quarterback	promotional				

pciovruyttid   _ r _ _ _ _ t _ v _ _ _

rertcpojo   _ _ _ j _ _ _ o _

ntriaoomolp   _ _ _ _ o _ i _ n _ _

ohpcyrpe   _ _ _ _ _ e _ y

otesdcuerp   p _ _ s _ _ u _ _ _

oonspsiriv   p _ o _ _ _ _ _ _ s

ciutybipl   p _ _ _ _ _ _ t _

qcauatberrk   _ _ _ r _ e _ _ _ _ k

ayierlt   _ _ _ _ _ t y

0. eecrde   r e _ _ _ _

. ecdvriee   _ _ c e _ _ _ _

2. rnniegtoico   r e _ _ _ _ _ t _ _ _

3. eeodncrmm   _ _ c _ _ _ e _ _

4. ucertri   R _ _ r _ _ _

Use at least 13 of your spelling words in a short creative story. Underline all spelling words used in the story.

Spelling Test

Your Answers	Correct Spelling If Incorrect
1	1
2	2
3	3
4	4
5	5
6	6
7	7
8	8
9	9
10	10
11	11
12	12
13	13
14	14
15	15
16	16
17	17
18	18
19	19
20	20

Use at least 11 of your spelling words in a short creative story. Underline all spelling words used in the story.

Spelling Test

Your Answers	Correct Spelling If Incorrect
1	1
2	2
3	3
4	4
5	5
6	6
7	7
8	8
9	9
10	10
11	11
12	12
13	13
14	14
15	15
16	16
17	17
18	18
19	19
20	20

Use at least 9 of your spelling words in a short creative story. Underline all spelling words used in the story.

_____

_____

_____

_____

_____

_____

_____

_____

_____

_____

_____

_____

_____

_____

_____

_____

_____

_____

_____

Extra Credit Spelling Words
Scramble

Name: _____

Date: _____

It's put your puzzle solving skills to the test. Try unscrambling the words using the words in the box.

remnants	rhinoceros	regulate	shepherd	rhythm	specialist
snowmobile	shirked	serene	semicircle	Specific	research
roommate	semicolon				

areltueg   _ _ _ u _ _ _ e   8. esooinmcl   _ _ m _ _ _ _ _ n

snmetnra   _ _ _ _ _ _ t s   9. erenes   _ e r _ _ _

heesarrc   _ _ s _ _ _ h   10. peshrdhe   _ _ _ _ _ e r _

renosroihc   _ _ i _ _ c _ r _ _   11. hkdseir   _ h i _ _ _ _

htymrh   r _ _ _ h _   12. oowimeblns   _ _ o w _ o _ _ _ _

oeamtrom   _ _ _ m m _ _ _   13. alpstceiis   _ p _ _ _ a l _ _ _

clreseiimc   _ _ m _ c _ _ c _   14. cefpiisc   S p _ _ _ _ _ _

Write sentences using words from above:

_____

_____

_____

Use at least 15 of your spelling words in a short creative story. Underline all spelling words used in the story.

Use at least 11 of your spelling words in a short creative story. Underline all spelling words used in the story.

Extra Credit Spelling Words
Scramble

Name: _____

Date: _____

et's put your puzzle solving skills to the test. Try unscrambling the words using the words in the box.

tamper	technician	straightedge	Traveled	toxic	successfully
subscription	suspended	threatening	trajectory	tragedy	technology
sulfur	submit				

stghiretadeg   _ t r _ _ _ _ t _ _ _ _

siumbt   _ _ _ m i _

sprtouscbnii   _ _ b s _ r _ _ _ _ _ _

fucucelyssls   _ _ _ c _ s s _ _ _ _ _

lurusf   _ _ l _ _ r

nusdedpes   _ _ _ _ e _ _ e _

parmet   t _ _ _ _ r

ecicnihnat   _ e _ _ n i _ _ _ _

gloecyhotn   _ _ _ h _ _ l _ _ y

). ngeehratnti   _ _ _ _ a t _ _ _ n _

. tcoix   t _ _ _ _

. rategyd   _ _ _ g _ _ y

. artotecrjy   _ _ _ _ _ c _ o r _

. dlravtee   T _ _ _ _ l _ _

Use at least 9 of your spelling words in a short creative story. Underline all spelling words used in the story.

Extra Credit Spelling Words
Scramble

Name: _____

Date: _____

Let's put your puzzle solving skills to the test. Try unscrambling the words using the words in the box.

Valedictorian	upright	unbelievable	tripod	unscathed	uncertainty
unicycle	typhoon	unconscious	unbreakable	trivial	utmost
urgent	unpredictable				

iotdpr   t _ i _ _ _

atrlvii   _ _ i _ i _ _

ypnthoo   t _ _ _ _ _ n

lnbuiveaeelb   _ _ _ e _ i e _ _ _ _ _

ebbuaelnark   _ _ _ _ e _ k a _ _ _

iernttnuacy   u _ _ e r _ _ _ _ _ _

cicnnsuuoso   _ _ _ _ n s _ _ _ u _

uycneicl   _ _ i _ _ _ _ e

bendairuletpc   _ _ _ r _ d _ _ t _ _ _ _

). nhueasctd   u n _ _ _ _ _ _ _

1. ptigurh   _ p _ _ _ h _

2. tnugre   u _ _ e _ _

3. stmotu   _ _ _ o s _

4. cdaarvtneilio _ _ _ _ _ i c _ _ r _ _ _

Use at least 14 of your spelling words in a short creative story. Underline all spelling words used in the story.

Spelling Test

Your Answers

1
2
3
4
5
6
7
8
9
10
11
12
13
14
15
16
17
18
19
20

Correct Spelling If Incorrect

1
2
3
4
5
6
7
8
9
10
11
12
13
14
15
16
17
18
19
20

Semester Planner

Week	Monday	Tuesday	Wednesday	Thursday	Friday
1					
2					
3					
4					
5					
6					
7					
8					
9					
10					
11					
12					
13					
14					
15					
16					
17					
18					

Notes

Class: _____

		Week:					Week:					Week:					Week:			
Day		M	T	W	Th	F	M	T	W	Th	F	M	T	W	Th	F	M	T	W	Th	F
Date																					
Assignments																					
Name																					
	1																				
	2																				
	3																				
	4																				
	5																				
	6																				
	7																				
	8																				
	9																				
	10																				
	11																				
	12																				
	13																				
	14																				
	15																				
	16																				
	17																				
	18																				
	19																				
	20																				
	21																				
	22																				
	23																				
	24																				
	25																				
	26																				
	27																				
	28																				
	29																				
	30																				
	31																				
	32																				

Semester Planner

Week	Monday	Tuesday	Wednesday	Thursday	Friday
1					
2					
3					
4					
5					
6					
7					
8					
9					
10					
11					
12					
13					
14					
15					
16					
17					
18					

Notes

Class: _____

		Week:					Week:					Week:					Week:			
Day		M	T	W	Th	F	M	T	W	Th	F	M	T	W	Th	F	M	T	W	Th	F
Date																					
Assignments																					
Name																					
	1																				
	2																				
	3																				
	4																				
	5																				
	6																				
	7																				
	8																				
	9																				
	10																				
	11																				
	12																				
	13																				
	14																				
	15																				
	16																				
	17																				
	18																				
	19																				
	20																				
	21																				
	22																				
	23																				
	24																				
	25																				
	26																				
	27																				
	28																				
	29																				
	30																				
	31																				
	32																				

Made in United States
Orlando, FL
16 March 2024

44836299R00063